Home Field

Ann Pilling

Ann Pilling

arrowhead
poetry

First published 2008 by
Arrowhead Press
70 Clifton Road, Darlington
Co. Durham, DL1 5DX
Tel: (01325) 260741

Typeset in 10 on 14pt Laurentian by
Arrowhead Press

Email: editor@arrowheadpress.co.uk
Website: http://www.arrowheadpress.co.uk

Printed by MPG Biddles Ltd., King's Lynn, Norfolk.

to my mother and father
who gave me poetry

Acknowledgements

Thanks are due to the editors of the following publications in which some of the poems in this book have appeared:

Acumen
Resource
Smiths Knoll
Staple
The North
Third Way

Growing Pains – Smith/Doorstop

Jacket Illustration:

Hay-cut Field
© 2008 Bob Gibbons / FLPA

Contents

A Field in Chardonnay

Somewhere in England a woman is reading 'Tess'
while on the edge of this small field I watch
a boy lay grass in curvy lines
and the blue of the sky is the blue of my old print dress.
I can see Hardy here as an old man wanting
that van towed away,
enragé as he stumps up the hill
spatted, cravatted, even in this blank heat,
counting his hard-earned acres at close of day.
Night drops, seeding its stars and the field
turns to that ashy hill where she pulled swedes
clawed them like skulls out of the hellish clay.

Always, in England, in anywhere, someone is crying
for the dawn and the rope and the flag, and the young girl dying.

Silent Noon

You doze, I listen.
In the spaces between songs an owl calls
from a Breton wood.
But these are English words, a poet writes
of golden kingcups
fringed with silver light; the trees edge nearer.

Where we shop for bread
the village square is filled with grey people,
stone sons, stone mothers,
squared off with a little fence. Here the war dead
are called *enfants*.
On Omaha Beach the waves turned red.

They still find shrapnel
buried in the sand but I can't take in
the scale of it all.
Is this music making me cry, or France,
or, from the sentinel trees, that lone owl's call?

August

Today's light lies lovely on the shaved fields, sloes
hang in the hedge like ear-drops as the clouds
stretch leisurely over their acres, curl up and stretch again
while the children pick little dry sticks from along the path
and run with them rattling white against white
along the baked margin till a stream of grass halts them
and they try to roll downhill
towards home, and the home field.

The Dingle

What was most lovely was its secretness
half a mile from town on our bikes, that last steep hill
taking our breath away when we braked and jumped off
chucking everything out to be first, no cautious lockings
or terrors about strange men, we were very little,
sarnies in greaseproof paper and bottles of pop.

I dare say trysts were kept there, babies got,
but we'd come for the leaping amongst its weathered rocks
for the fishing in its clean shallows,
sun pushing down through intense shade
patched on its forest floor like puddles of ink.
It was sweet there, the smells especially were sweet,
fern smell and smell of the water, deep as wine.

It's a mean place now, council boulders clog the chained paths down,
the rim's crusted with houses, our feet crunch litter.
I need my son's son with me today
to take my hand and dance with me under its shrunk light.
It is time to grow into my childhood.

To a Tree

I'm worried about you, you let go your leaves
too fast this time, savagely.
Like an old maid with a hated virginity
at a stroke you got rid.

Old woman you're shrinking. Everything's dropped down
to that bulge round your sagging trunk
three feet up from the pavement as if
what's left of you has pooled and is draining
into a sump underneath your thick elephant foot,
ridged and more stone than wood already,
a mallet would send chips flying.

Don't go yet, you were good to me
those weeks I was stuck in this bed.
Mornings you greeted me, I loved
your big-bear Autumn coat, I loved
your spiny, concerned peep through my window when,
sleepy last thing, I shut you out for the night,
you were always back, first light.

Give me one more spring.

Jodi's People

All week Auschwitz has been remembered
in grainy footage of stick people
hillocks of shoes, ovens blowing their tops
and cattle trucks (how did the cattle feel?)

They recalled Auschwitz this week
in prayers, naming the dead very slowly,
in poems recited by children.

This week at the Auschwitz site there was singing
a steady tonguing of lament
in which all but the stunned birds joined.

But only today in my friend's white room
hearing Kaddish played on that rough violin
raw with the plangency of some dying animal
did grief become a single note
to which everything in me joined

and I opened my mouth then for those I had never known,
Gunter and Eloise and Hans,
and Jodi's people.

The Archives
(for my father)

A postcard from a niece on honeymoon in Greece
a grainy photo black and white, of rain on an old shed
'It's cold' she writes 'But our love keeps us warm'.
An e-mail from a friend to tell me Fred
will never speak again, if he survives –
two more for the archives.

What will they do with this when our light fails, with the piles
of boxes, mainly black, a couple red, that make
two teetering columns on the floor
of the back attic, cosying up
to a budgie cage , to those
unlucky peacock drapes which Pam
threw at me once, thinking I meant her harm.
Will they warm, the after-people,
to how year after year I lugged up here
the detritus of lives
sons, lovers, wives,
a child's splodge here, a holed pot there, a pair
of tiny corded shorts, a coin collection
spilled on the rafters now for mouse inspection.

Daddy, I laughed at your hoardings, now I'm you.

Programme Notes

We are the little people who care about dust.
Before writing our poem (usually a sonnet) the paper
is lined up neatly parallel to the writing desk and the pencils
laid out in rows, like guardsmen.

Beethoven, his stiff black hair cut spikily
probably with butchers' scissors
awaited the young Czerny who
puzzled to see the maestro's ears stopped up with yellow cotton
scrambled over a year's debris to the sinking piano
where, for a while, his teacher listened patiently
then played himself, and spoke with the living God.

Piano

All the dead bones
rise and present themselves vertical
like that just-discovered wreck on the ocean floor
and in her face
framed by the music stand and the piano's lid
I see your face.

Evening. Notes trickle through the house
Chopin and Liszt and the Schubert Impromptu
she played as encore. Her lips
softened then, something round the eyes eased
and I saw your prettiness, your small hands
move over the keys like flittering moths,
all your dead bones
singing and dancing.

Here's One They Made Earlier

Here's one they made earlier, a Fifties child,
the giveaway is the candy-striped school frock
the clomping shoes and the hair in those funny clumps
(she's cut off her plaits so she can be George in the Famous Five
she's hoping for shorts).

Someone scampers across the grass.
She pockets her secateurs, uncreaks her knees,
he wants full attention. His Harry outfit
is silk-lined gorgeously, his specs
are state of the art but he needs
her steady hand with the kit that will give his forehead
its magical scar.

She limps after him
thinking of George and of how, those days,
it was all in the mind.

Daredevil

Sent upstairs for being bad
slobbing it up on the school bus
cheeking Dad,
but I wasn't bothered, I liked
being under the roof.

You could hear rain up there,
and birds, a plane
lumbering north towards Burtonwood,
Yanks in it, the same
fabulous brown men who chucked us chewing gum
sailing serenely through gardens, their fat funnels
topping the trees.

Best was the balcony
two foot square,
ornament only
but I squeezed out there
to spy
forty foot down on the stick people,
dangling my hair
for a man to leg up it and set me free.

I still like heights
and drops, still stand
too near the thick white line, still nudge
closer and closer to the cliff's edge
still feel
my mother's hand pulling me back.

Here

a boy glides down a corridor on wheeled shoes
calculates finely when he must swerve to the left,
turn his back on the window with its crashing sea.
He heads off into the gloom of wardrobes,
Grandmother's wheel-chair, half a bike, his lips
are those of angels in the Uffizi.
His mother sleeps, her hair
glistens like blackberries on stems hung with rain.
She peers at me from a photo,
two years old and in her father's arms.
In the cold of the morning
I sit on the balcony with some tiny chairs.

Nearly Walking

He stands by his blue truck, observes its shininess,
and with intense deliberation flings
a shower of hens and sheep upon the floor
watching their fall through space and measuring
the speed and impact of each separate piece.

He's nearly walking and his mother phones
with news of his first stab
at staying upright. Tremulous in air
I see him sway about, testing the spring
of ottoman and chair before
reliably collapsing on the breast
of the flat's cool walls
serene and white and solid where he zooms
at fifty miles an hour towards the kitchen.

I want him not to walk but to remain
caught in this miracle where time has stopped
and all is space and light-motes in the air
and carouselling colours from the street
where postmen call and pubmen roll their beer
and girls trip by with bags and little dogs.

But the map's in place.
I cannot change the pattern of the stars
or stop the birds from flying to the south
or freeze the lily's sword which, in the window,
proclaims itself a necessary flower
after so many years of waiting green.

Walking With George

With George all puddles are approached
with reverent slowness and the feet applied
perfectly flat for biggest splash. It seems
a dirty gum-stuck pavement is preferred
to whorling Yorkshire slabs steam-cleaned to honey
by men in orange hats. With chewing gum
his shoes can measure their bionic powers
and he his own self may decide which blob's
America, and which the sea. In Bedford Gardens
a hot sky sizzles cobalt-blue, roped thick
with creamest blossom, garlanding the street
like bunting. Small birds strafe the avenue
with twigs and pelt the ear with song. His small
egg-speckled nose lifts high, sniffing the air. This white
could be anything: snow, icing, last night's duvet
pulled over our heads to make a dragon's cave.
His hand in mine is flower-soft, he leads me
with shining face tip-tilted to the bright
enormous sky down paths I never knew
before this day, or thought I had forgotten.

Prayer Before Birth

Last night it was talk about children, in the pub
the air grew thick as lines from MacNeice's
Prayer Before Birth snaked up our table legs
flickering unease. Today from this room
the view's brilliant, the land all flowing
in lovely lines, paint on wet paper, grey
lynchets pleating the meadow, sheep
dotting the grass like mushrooms while one wall
seals off their field in case
all colour runs off the page. The straight
lines of this house have turned fluid, the walls
have started to belly out, and we're birthed
into the bright exterior where we walk
willing this big blue river to flow
into the child's new blood , this tree-wind
to be the first music it hears.

One Christmas

One Christmas hangs in memory like lamps
in a deep wood, the year the village band
chugged up our hill in an old van and set up
over the road in a gateway. Their forest green
jackets were snibbed with silver, cornets and tubas
slicing the dark like moons, and what looked like flowers,
white flowers blooming in winter, turned out to be sheep
jockeying for position as the word got round.

Later I went out for coal and heard, floating up from Keld,
Away in a Manger, misty on the night air.
The sheep hadn't budged from the gate but the flock had spread
a great wing over the fell as it stood there listening,
stone-still, waiting for the next move.

Miscarried

Nothing changes. Your big man's voice,
grave on the shifting air, narrows my heart
like a child crying. These days your large fingers
quite bury mine, enclosing my whole hand
as a nut wraps its kernel.

The call over, I go dumbly about, rooting among pockets
for some little *bouchée* of sweetness, for some ointment
to rub on the angry place, tearing up cotton
for an important bandage. I climb the stairs
always feeling behind me
to catch your trailing hand.

When you are sleeping
I'll fetch my book and camp outside your room
to keep giants away.

After Weeping

When you are in pain I want you back inside me
blindly fed and warmed, enduring nothing worse
than my heart's steady beat.
I was all in all to you then and would be again,
the cord was never cut.

Now you're a woman help me to take shears to it
or we'll be like Russian nesting dolls
your child in you, you in me, all of us locked in,
air excluded, no fire let out to burn.

One image of God is like this, good and bad together,
the tie that binds and the gold cord loosed,
strangleholds, knots.

Aeroplanes
(for Francesco)

Bird-like (for those who made them studied birds
watching them climb the air as they drove upwards
though carelessly, as if the air were nothing) these jets
pencil the air aslant and disappear
into their puffy counterpanes of cloud.

No more is seen until they perch again
on sand or concrete flats or sunny town
or in the place to which I fly this night,
a sad grey city washed with bitter rain.

The Elephant's Coat

(for Francesco)

All summer he has bedded patiently
with the toys that mound the foot of our hall stair,
with a lump of fur that might have been a dog,
with a clock that winds and plays a little tune
under the real clock from which, and inexplicably,
you sometimes turn away your face.

This dapper little jumbo
could be snoozing now in any club in London
except that some old retainer, courteously,
would have restored his coat, the scrap of felt
you prised off while still in nappies
to see what was underneath.

We fit it together, me explaining about frost,
and you absolutely understand that
now the year darkens and the cat
makes its hot nightly circle on my feet this lord of the jungle
must be kept warm, just as you understand
that we must pull *no more stuffing* from the feet of the big clown who
with his awful lolling head presides in the kitchen corridor
over boxes of blocks and a tiny flotilla of cars,
the real sword.

Breakfast

I like the morning best because the day's
untrodden like a field of quiet snow.
The birds are morning people. I don't care
if their bright chatter's territorial
and warning other fellers off their patch,
to me it speaks of hope and joyous days,
their sense that all the world is here for them.

At breakfast Franco surfs his usual shelves
for Coco-pops and waffles, eggy toast,
as if these humdrum possibilities
were shiny new and born again today.

For him the golden edge will not be dulled
when letters come, or callers, or when Grandpa
shoves off into his room and Granny sides
dishes into the sink and starts again.

Lapped in a pool of quiet he contemplates
his shadow, jabs it, queries Peter Pan
and asks why Hulk is green while in the garden
we harvest dark globes from the raspberry trees.
It's always breakfast to a little child.

Nonna

I played Gran to her Nonna. Both too idle
to learn the other's tongue we talked
in pidgin French about him, *qu'il était
formidable*, his first words, when he first walked.

Now she lies dead in an upper room. The sun
shines on her lion face, her mane of hair.
One hand cups her cheek. The men in the road
have clean white shirts. He has seen her there.

Below a forest grows of weeping trees.
He pushes through legs to a screen, with a gun
zaps monsters cold. Someone takes tea to the police.
We close ranks when the undertakers come.

Death won't hit him like this again.
These walls, this air,
the picture of the woman lying there
are graved on his inward eye. They have entered
the pores of his skin.

Pullman's God

He died some time ago. Did they
suck him up with the Dyson or is he
out in the back with the Christmas tree
ready to go to the dump? He died
not with a bang but a whimper; here we stand
toasting the New Year on twin Oxford hills
the glass half-full, half empty.

Give me uncertainty, give me
that ravishing dawn I saw last week when the sky
split open over Fremington Edge and the blood
ran down. Give me
the silence of the cataract ward when my friend came round
saw men like the trees walking
then saw them whole. Give me
the way Francesco rocked to see his stocking filled
and his wordless fingering of that letter from St Nicholas
in its crabbed, kind hand.

The Cooling Towers near Sheffield

Big-bellied, calm, they stand against the wind
like ships that take on sail
where the road rises and the land fills up
with factories and junkyards. Always I hope for a stop
for roadworks or for some poor slithering lorry
to shed its load so that, all engines off,
I can look properly.

They are liquid in summer, the heat comes up at them
like waves of shimmering corn, they are great stooks
the last in the meadow, Mother and Father to us
big gods tipping the sky, their castled tops
whimsically different, the work of some bored apprentice
on a cathedral roof.

I love their swelling. I want to climb inside
into their furred blackness, falling and falling like Alice,
or snuggle against their backs like a child in bed.

But will men come soon lugging a great machine?
Will they topple and die at last and be carted away
while from under their crumpled skirts the mice go running
into the darkness that stains the outer ring?

Black

West of Manchester privets were blacker
and thicker, the birds bounced off them
like trampolines and they didn't grow they were more
hacked out of something like
the furred black walls of my school. I thought
the stones for that came from the ground black
till I watched quarry men planing big blocks and saw
that the colour was gingery, mild as milk.
Gran said our little lungs were black too.

There was green in Wales but black crept after us,
holiday summers, my white room
cold as a cell, at night the black
torn only by owls, me start-eyed missing
the night-song of buses as the dream journey
slid me down terrifying rails to a Hades where
the miner chewed all day on his sweet green shoot defying
black to be all there is.

Home Town

Where I came from the houses
were all black and I liked this black because I liked
precise and definite things
right angles, pencils
ordered like guardsmen in immaculate rows
and my top sheet
turned back perfectly parallel
to the pillow's edge.

I didn't know then
that this black was spewed out of chimneys, that
the stones of our house had started off honey
before the smoke got them. Funny

how my black period's become grey
awash with possibilities
lacking sharp focus.

Mr. Ashton

Mr. Ashton delivered our coal and he must have been diminutive
because I, not waist-high to my little mother then,
considered him small. His square thick body
packed a terrific punch, he would stagger,
the bags hung double over his leather back,
carapaced tortoise-fashion along our path,
he was always singing or roaring.

His load, best cobbles and nutty slack,
fountained into the coalhouse with a great whoosh
and while the black dust settled our mother paid him
with grubby pound notes and they cracked jokes.
In his black face his mouth looked like a chop, his broken teeth
stunningly white. His hands were black
and the fur on his arms was black and the great black
of his roaring with my mother went on and on.

I thought he was Satan because,
at that time, I was praying to God a lot
and the thing I feared most was the actual flames of hell,
but I loved Mr. Ashton.
With his shiny tortoise back and his blackness he made
my little mother laugh.
If there is heaven
let Mr. Ashton be there.

White Out

After a day's hard stare how sweet it is
to turn one's face away, switch on the dark
and tumble feather-bedded down a slope
of perfect white to where the shimmering sky's
one whirl of down from an old mother's plucking
her everlasting chicks. In last week's blizzard
I thought of her and of our town's drab winters
and how we shrieked when its grey snow was sticking.

Half conscious in this thinning light I breathe
sweet gas, its light-green apple smell, and feel
a mask over my face, then the dentist man
who smiles and offers me a bloody tooth
and Mummy is there and I am very brave
and do not cry until the door is shut
of my small toppling front of attic room
whose grinning bookshelves hold the devil in.

Why did our mother paint those edges red?
Why did I search in vain for Peter Pan
and find instead the History of the Rod
and poems that I did not understand
and yet I did? Coming awake at last
it is as if nothing bad has ever happened
no-one is dead and this white counterpane
is the untrodden snow of all my life.

The Lepers

That Christmas we got leprosy they all
shunned us because of what you'd done
and every line went dead. They left
things on the step, little notes, flowers,
even a pie, but nobody rang the bell
except Brown from the church who Daddy screamed away
beefing him shit-scared down the path.

                            Each year
the smells come back, earth, gas, the brown-bread smell
of Auntie's house, and feelings, how all food
stuck half way down my throat like something hooked
on a bent nail.

It was cold when you died, they used special cutters
to start that small black hole they dropped you in.
I still see it, the grubby back-cloth of the town
the uncles and the tall priest
curved over your grave like rooks.

My First Bra

I'd like to think my mother bought it for me
and with me for that matter since it was I
who had to get into the thing
but I can't be sure, she seemed
to disapprove of breasts being flattish herself
and that they were all my fault.

I think she bought me sanitary towels
but only the once then, in her vague mysterious way,
went off to read a life of Gladstone
or play the piano or hide
beautiful unnecessary objects in our damp cellar
in case Father found them and shouted.

She seemed to forget
that menstruation could last for forty years
and the pain of life (*listen*, she turned on the gas when I was just nineteen)
the pain of life for ever.

Dead Letter

You were so little, a warm brown thing
with a warm bread smell. The day you died
I slept in your bed. What I liked best
was fitting the curve of your back to the curve of my front.
I could hear your heart beat.

I didn't write before. What you did
was terrible. Its larval ash
swirls on and on, still burns people.
Sometimes it brands them.
You should see our faces.

Today though I just feel love
and there's something to show you,
a picture of the man I married.
That's us cutting the cake, he guides
the beribboned knife, his hand
on top of mine.

It's a small hand, he's a small man.
He tells rude jokes chucking
his head back like you did
then laughing and laughing. He's got
your eyes and your quiet
Lancashire voice.
Mummy, I married you.

The Removal

Leaving the place
was like watching you die, the same coldness, the same
unblemished walls scrubbed clean, the same
dull sense of something very slowly going home.

Bunched in a corner of its last scoured cell
like a last spider, I could dimly see
tables and chairs being manoeuvred out,
bed-ends, a sofa, Mother's china dogs
and our black parlour grand stuck in the doorway,
nearly lifting the roof off like a crust.

Out in the road there was chat
as all was muffled into swaddling clothes
for the new journey, then a final rattle
when on the hill some tall wheels took a bend.

Nothing to stay for then but hunkered down
on the bare tiles I waited,
fluff curling round the floor like baby's hair,
because the breathing of the house had stopped
with no-one left to let its spirit free
but me, its chatelaine.

This new not being
lay heavy like the imprint of a hand
on hardening clay, a nib
etching itself on silence.

As when bells cease to chime in summer's air
leaving the greater part of sound behind
in the space they have quitted.

Window

First light and the familiar street
is big with snow, her fingernail
furrows through frost flowers making safe passage
for Israelites as the sea
foams up and suspends.

By noon the pane streams tears, she can hardly see
the house over the road, its curtained front room,
the black stick people coming and going
are wobbly lines, their round hats mopheads.

Dusk and thick wings crack the glass.
She peers down through a crazed V and watches
a long car slow and stop outside their door.

FROM THE ANTIPODES

In Flight

On my personal TV screen a map
charts our continuous progress and the plane
has a wing-span the length of New Zealand with a red
line coming out of its backside
stiff, like a strained rope. Regular bulletins
tell us how many miles we are from Mecca
and at each take-off
a prayer is said to Allah for safe journeys,
May our time be shortened
May we see no bad sights.

Girls bring us nuts and mango juice
their sleepy eyes like sloes and Australia
looks like a lot of grey dust. I'm reading *Voss*,
he's started to cross the desert and they're already
eating their mules and shooting their dogs.

Nobody's died yet.

At Binna Burra

There's only colour where light penetrates and then
it's the mad green of ferns house high,
spreading their chic umbrellas, underfoot
plums roll like small blue marbles and there are
orange grape clusters, little as peas. The path,
shallowly graded for tourists, is plaited
with the long dried tongues of eucalyptus leaves.
A bird makes the sound of a whip and a face
meets mine, doe-eyed but perky, relaxing on long feet.
Sue says it's a pademelon, a little marsupial.
We exchange stares.

Birdcalls lessen as we go deeper, this forest
has its own life. I freeze when the easy path
is suddenly striped by a thing as thick as my arm, some black
gloss thing is barring the way with its dragon scales,
and it's over a metre long. Not rushing
it slides off and I see
another black shadow bigger than me melting
into a curious patch of tingling yellow light.

The place is indifferent to us but we feel followed.
Here the first people
smoothed weapons to glass with the rough-grained leaves
of this sandpaper fig. Look, it can make you bleed. Are all
these trails an affront? As we step out
onto the safe, tarred road the trees
draw their black curtains over our human act.

Wilderness

'No camping on this beach, no barbecues,
dog owners take all faecal matter home.'
So I turn my back on the board and its snug letters
cut deeply in, well-spaced, ochre on green.
The sand's yolk-yellow and the Tasman ocean
broken in glassy chunks by some black spars,
a half-dead tree that someone set on fire,
like a stag with broken knees, its antlers frame
the sea in shiny droplets flecked with white.

I dream they're Mother's eardrops split with pearls.
The swell gets big, mates with the wind outside,
goes surging through my veins, hot blue.

New Zealand

A rust-red truck nosed like a dolphin snoozes
in the corner of a field which is perfectly square
and packed with sheep all pointing one way
like wall to wall carpeting. This truck's
not going anywhere, it has already taken on
the colours of grass and sky, and of that mountain
sticking its chin over the fence its head
suddenly furred with snow.

Displaced Persons

What's wrong? You're with me and that phone call
wasn't from England and about a death.
Why am I planning now
an assault on the patio moss in our winter garden
here where the sun
beats down on us and on this good bread?

Those vines are the clue,
those strangler figs we saw at Binna Burra.
Starting from the top
where a bird's smeared clean its beak from the tacky fruit
they grow downwards, latticing the mother trunk
and weave cathedral fans till the quick of it
blackens and dies.

                    You're right
I can't write about love, only about vines.
Grimly attached to my Northern Hemisphere,
growing steadily down, they've had
a lifetime to get rooted.

Kay

i.

'It's not Kay,' I said to her boy
'It's a container', and I touched her hard face
chilled from a mortuary drawer, its mouth
hurriedly closed, for the viewing. The skin
was pearly, like fat on ham. In Ireland
they used to open windows when a person died
and I once saw a bed in a museum
with a slit in its rose-pink tester
to let the soul go free.

ii.

The curtains are drawn in my house, and the long blinds,
and in the dark the chairs and tables wait
and you are dead. Do you remember
when we were little girls, that neighbour knocking?
Jean, it was spinster Jean with the bent mouth,
her mother hung behind, white as a cup. 'Don't let
the children peep when Father's coffin comes,'
spitting the words like stones. They must have hated
our terrible garden, the cat shit, bikes, shirts
stuck on the line after a three day frost. When they'd gone
our little mother cried. They sat in for weeks,
they never saw her tidying, that blue cedar
she put in the back border, the spring bulbs. Their curtains
stayed shut as faces.

See,
I have made an inch of sun in mine,
to let the flowers breathe.

iii.

I've got my magic knickers on, they make
my funeral coat look good,
thin me down to a line,
give me height. I step out bravely
sing all the hymns, don't cry, my steady arms
hold weeping people up.

When it's over and I lie down
my globs of flesh come back,
ease themselves over belly and thigh,
like slugs regaining ground , my throttled
little-girl cry swells to a scream, this tide
I've swept back all day
becomes a tsunami.

41

iv.

Now you are ash
we tip you into a hole under the small prunus
but first I hold you to me. You are in
a long tub with your name on
in a red bag tied with tassels,
it could be your dressing gown. The roundness
feels like a body. I hug it for a long time.

Now you are dead
memories stalk me like mountains, that four poster
we trampolined on, lying
side by side like hairpins before rolling
into the dinge of the mattress,
snuggling up. I don't know
if this feel of a body at night is yours or our mother's
or that of a child that has fallen asleep against me.

v.

Did you come to this house when you lived in Ireland?
it's early, nobody's here yet.
I can picture Austen women dancing on the perfect lawn
it's like a film set.

Flowers
stipple the grass , speedwell and violet, anemone gone wild,
these hedge mosaics
remind me of Wales. You were the child
who filled leaf bowls with berries
let spiders run over your hands while I screamed.

The damp
of this cellar kitchen
is the damp of the room we slept in, every summer
we ravished it like a tomb.

Now you are all
folded away like sheets.
I must keep to the very margin of this bright field
it's cold out of the sun.

Phone Home

She's dead and I want to ring home so I pick up a phone
and it starts to grow big in my hand, my nails
root for a footing like on a cliff's edge, fingers
piston out numbers and I hear
this far-off shrilling, like wind through wire.

She's dead and I want to crawl down the phone
be a worm in its gut burrow into her but
she's under the earth now, people say
that hair goes on growing, that fingernails curve
right round in tight circles, the black
stains of the corpse will have spread now
but I don't care. I want to kiss those lips.

They buried her under big trees and I'm here and the phone
bleats uselessly inside an empty house.
There'll be nothing but silence now and the words
I never said and over her head
the thin, pointed mockery of the birds.

Lump

I won't die of this, even so
I plan to arrange my thoughts as for the end
and take things with me when they put me under
like treasures in a tomb.

George sawing off the kitchen door knob,
grave in his fireman's suit, that swim
me and the Swale and three new ducks
like humbugs in the water, those warm pebbles
stroking my back, the first words ever
to make me cry up in my attic room
'Balder the beautiful is dead, is dead.'

Breasts

They have done the state some service and they know it
suckled my boys, pleasured my man,
now they have to go under the knife.

I'm being good to them I've bought
fine cottons pricked with little flowers,
I bathe them in sweet oils and I no longer
sit like a hunchback cramming them from sight.

Why in my fat-girl days did I wear bags
to hide their lovely roundness? Why did I
mound them with cushions on our old settee?

In water they float out like lily pads
nippled with dark pink buds as this old river
creeps silently to its weir. Sad I've denied them, sad
how love, released, runs wild when it is too late.

Mr. B

He's glossy, racehorse sleek, each day
his wife must pour him into his suit and fix his tie.
When he opens the door everyone falls back
parting to let him through, like the waves of the Red Sea.

He's such a busy person, snip here, chop there,
and he goes round the ward like a whisk
perching on beds, swishing curtains till
quite suddenly he sprints away.

'I'll see her at ten,' and he nods in my direction,
but he won't will he? I'll be
under by then, all he'll see
framed in green cloth is a felt-tipped bit of me.

I'm awake by four and I distinctly hear
Nurse Clark take a message from Mr. B's wife,
change of time for their supper date. His knife
is slicing Elsie's breasts off as she jots it down.

Elsie's old, I've watched her
drink in his words like cooling water,
she's that woman in the Bible who touched Christ's hem

                                        But then
what can it be like, to be Mr. B, what must
sex be like, and eating, and always having
to make a distinction between
our various bits of breast and the messed
up meat on his plate tonight, at the dinner party?

Sweating at Arvon

These nights of sweat well suit
the pig sty room I write my poems in,
one in a line, slant roofed, I bet
they sloshed the swill out where my bed is.

I sweat at twelve, at three, and then again
at five, and the pigness of pigs
blankets me in a dark pink heat. I don't know
if pigs sweat, if a pig's inner thermostat
sometimes goes mad like mine, but I need
pig nakedness, humble and unashamed.

Before sweats it was breasts. They
measured them, poked at them, beamed
their shiny Starwars machines at them, I became
all breast, and numbers, and a date of birth.

This room's home now, I can smell
its steady centuries of loved pigs, hear
their companionable rooting, picture
a sow slumped down on my bedside rug
like a big bolster hemmed
with ten identical pink lozenges, watch
ten pert embroidered tails quiver in ecstasy.

On Being Sixty

The balloons have drifted slowly up to the top of the house
where they nudge the ceiling and hover
like people waiting for a lift to open.
On Saturday they were full to bursting,
fat fruits ripe at the year's turning,
But they sag now.

Above our roof the sky's that tingling blue
of late October, homing birds etched black
in little lines, each cloud hand-picked.

They are bumping the rafters now
the sky's the thing
to be out there, to be carried across the world
on the thin, fine air, to get strength again
be more balloon than they were before.

Let me open the window.
One more push and we'll be away.

The Shared Cat

With you he's a lover, climbing your leg
in a complicated way like someone
going the wrong way up a fire escape, he never
stays long with me or locks himself
into my married rhythm, he knows
you're on your own.
I'm one of the pack, he's tuned in
to the way I lie awake, ears cocked,
always listening for the front door.

And both of us will suddenly bound off
for our own reasons, him
because of sudden noises and delicious smells, me
because someone is calling to me from a distant place
someone
I thought long gone away.

Burying Zebedee

It's death again. Now, side by side,
we push spades into mellow earth
setting him gently down in the mild ground.

We have turned up shooting bulbs that should be snowdrops,
somewhere a blackbird sings above our heads,
it is quite warm, so near the Saviour's birth.

We heap up soil and strew a few brown leaves,
light shades the grass. Suddenly it is hateful.
Why does the sun have to shine when we bury the dead?
It is as if everything has to go on somehow
when for us it has come to a stop.

Always the same thing happens to the body
the craw turns hard and the face freezes
nothing goes down.
In the slow curve in which he has set
we see ourselves mirrored.

It is not as if we have been allowed to love him,
He was always alone, always stealing off somewhere
on his mysterious ways.
Yes, he was beautiful but I wanted more return
for what we had given.

I follow you into the house
soon we will light our candles.
May the Lord when he comes
find his people watching and waiting.

Lullay, Zebedee.
You were this year's lesson in love
and a lesson in grace.

Dunlins

(for Michael Longley)

They might have gone already, that grey line
which separates dull sky from duller grass
could be a thread of mist, but it is water
a ribbon fringed with chattering migrants.
They fly up as we edge nearer and go east
in a single streak towards St Barnabas,
skirt the campanile then swarm back
in the shape of a wide stole,
cloud yellow flecked with black
like drift from a bonfire. After that first wing surge
they are silent, they have stopped over our heads
frozen in air, watching the conductor. But we can see
the child's tick of each bird continuously flapping
to keep its position in the dance,
as in a poem, where every word must work
to earn its place.

Port Meadow, with Geese

Over our heads the small birds fly in skeins,
thin out, gather again then bunch together
as if someone is waving the corner of a great silk.
Going higher they narrow almost to a single line
then turn over, their bellies whitening the thick sky
and we hear a dry clatter of wings, like sticks taking hold.

At the rim of the land, casually smudged in,
brown lines that could have been dung or irrigation ridges
obligingly separate, becoming geese.
Always at this dead time
they rest here on their haul from the cold countries.

We are looking across a sea of quiet birds,
each arranged with circumspection in its own large oval,
as if already dressed, prepared for table on a platter,
until one shifts and walks forward wagging its broad rump
and rocks, old woman fashion.

We do not see them go, but in the night
they fly across the eye of my mind,
one long dark jag against an intense sun,
and I think of the man who got wings and became a god
and who flew in ecstasy above the tumbling planet,
not seeing how the hedges enclosed its neat, patched fields
or its little divisions of land, or the lines
ruled out between men, and nations.

Spring Lamb

Yes and they do spring, away from us as we squeeze through a stone slit
and drop into their meadow, away from dogs
and from the head-butting of ewes not theirs.
From where we stand they're soap-flake white, cloud puffy
but sink your hand in, it's like pan-scrubbers, yellowy,
tails dangling down in little lumps. Why do these innocents
leap off the minute a boot crushes their new grass? Is it
noise, smell, big teeth inside
a fat red mouth, or have they seen
the shape of long knives slid out of sight
cosy against warm shins?

Ceide Fields

'The men were short, their women even shorter,
five foot probably, the men not more than five foot six,
you can tell this from their graves,
and they must have believed in something
because these were very grand, very serious tombs.
To make their houses they cut down their trees
And that is why, perhaps, the bog came back.'
And why they left this place, these fabulous flat cliffs
dropping sheerly and architecturally down into the black sea
off the coast of Mayo.

When it was dark they went obediently to sleep.
I do not think their dreams would have greatly troubled them
or that they made love with the aid of mirrors
or that they feared the mental darkness coming up like a tide
or that they might turn into their mothers.
Their god too was a simple affair, a mere shaft of stone.
It stands there still, footed with gorse and heather,
saying 'I am the God of comfort. There is no other.'

Iona Snapshot

This little boat
moored to its bobbing orange on a shiny sea
centres the frame. Above, a strip of blue
then sand, dark white, that crumbles in my hand
like couscous. Green then, where the sheep graze and then my feet
steadying my body as I take the shot.

It is safe here and we have safely swum
always in sight, beyond our narrow bay,
of a great water, hearing always too
bird cries that thrill us, though bird busyness
has no play with us swimmers and our thoughts.

It is the interior that terrifies,
these tiny hills benign with flocks
create a pressure, the heat is too intense
the sky too blue and we can hardly breathe.

Here's the confusion of the inland path
where the knots tighten, roots as thick as arms
make our feet trip, sly creepers
wrap necks and ankles in a stranglehold.

Only when we have found our bay again
do we breathe easier. Seeing the boat
orders interior space, the long
fingers of sand dig in the dampening beach
for the necessary cold, the sharp
cry of the gulls reminds us of his call.

The Wave

came suddenly and took great life, sent bones
of houses skittering along the perfect beach like leaves,
perched ships on roofs, spiked trees with bloody arms and legs,
pulped faces featureless on paradisal sand.

We are the postcards now, me walking
in English fields, my Christmas muffler
bloodsplashed against the neutral greys
of barn and wall and snug toy field where sheep
group trustfully under their home fell
jaunty in its cap of white.

But at night the pod of sleep bursts open and I'm out there
checking the hills through our window, seeing the wave
stalk like a mountain over this quiet land.

Missing

There is no sea here
only the black pool
appalling now as I look for you in vain
up by the waterfall.

There are no cliffs here
only the yellowing rocks
of an inland valley
old men's teeth
smoothed by the Swale.

Here moorland birds
flap up from bitten grass
sometimes a gull cries
strangled, a foreigner.

I think then of wastes of sea
of pebbles roaring as the tide goes home.
Missing is like the undertow,
its slow grinding, the rush
of amber water over these stones.

In the night I think of drowning
and my mouth opens in that harsh gull cry
till water stops it.

I am afraid then, want not to be,
but I do not sleep. Always
the sharp pebbles pull back
drawing blood
then tears.

After These Years

I look across the sea, the sea of Marmora,
it is cold and the glass misty, in the bay
an ugly boat slides by.
But we have seen this day the gorgeous palaces
as we squelched through mud then rocked home cheerfully
on broken pavements, snuggled together for warmth.
So we have sailed to Byzantium, you and I.

I look across the sea, the sea of years,
to when we sought and clutched each other's hands
and moved away from the old familiar shore
and struck out for a place we'd never seen
and would not know unless we trod together
that cold, uncertain sea.
Nothing, my dear, was less like freezing ocean
than knowing you.

I look across the sea, dark now, and calmer as the night
unfolds its peace and in that peace I see
your lips, your gentle hands,
your fabulous face.

If you should die before I die
I'll get them to sing Ella
and I'll think of how you cried at the sentimental
but at the great things too.
And I'll get them to read George Herbert
because you have been to me his seasoned timber
his sweet and virtuous soul that never gives.

I look across the sea where, among tangled mastheads,
a boy once swam and turned into a god.
So, in the hands of God, ordinary water
became an everlasting spring.
And so our love.

59

Edward Hopper

The lighthouse and the lighthouse house
are almost consumed by the dark foreland and the sky
is deepest azure, thickening towards the top of the frame
where a cloud is caught on some lighthouse detail
(possibly a balcony)
like a feather, perfectly horizontal.

                    He said
sunlight was always white
unless towards early morning or
towards the close of the day
and should never be painted yellow.

In the film,
at the end of his life, his good tweed jacket
swallows him like a sack,
he is a death's head, silent, waiting,
as the people in his pictures are waiting.

Thaw

Snow light is big, like sea light, you know
something has happened, when you were in bed
or dozing in the back of a car. It feels different.

It snowed in this room, the white
of my sheet met the wall's white, a brilliance
plucked my eyes open and there was
a silence on me that was not familiar
like the wrong coat. It is intense
this quiet of snow
like silence after music.

But already, while I'm still wondering
how it feels to be all white,
to be like swans or angels, the roof opposite
crumples and falls with a thud into the street
setting off fat flakes
that shake themselves from the privets
like a dog just out of the river.

Shock Treatment Scene

When they start tightening the straps I shut
my eyes and ram my longest fingers home
into the pupils till it hurts. I put
(neatly, because I'm practised) my right thumb
against its corresponding ear and then
my left, there are no cracks, these rounds
of flesh might have been made for this and when
I look again it's finished. Music sounds
we seek the street and find a place to sit.
I drink and talk but not of those who pass
tormented through my brain. My fingers fit
like clustered organ pipes around my glass
snug and complete, with no sly chinks that might
admit the cruel, arbitrary light.

White Easter

I am looking at the door of your room,
how the inside timbers make a cross, how that black knob
could be a nail head. You are ill behind it.

Snow caps the fell. We should get up there,
walk the Good Friday walk, but you sleep on
under your white mound. One hand makes an air-hole.

Day Two Christ harrows Hell and I've become
a widow in my mind, tearing sheets into grave cloths.
Why didn't we get lambs' blood, to smear our doorposts?

Sunday the outside whiteness is complete
with the sheep brown against it. I hear hymns, you showering.
I take up my position on the blue stairs
wait for the pair of you to burst forth.

Swaledale

Its long body comforts me. I lie along it sometimes
warming myself against its soft hills burying
my face in the hair of its trees, the sheep
are pointilliste against its ribbed fells
its groined hushes. At dusk the valley
clasps me in strong hands.

The Attack

This day a year ago your heart faltered
and there are pictures in my mind, that yard
behind the house where they backed in, two men
red-faced like jolly farmers, the thin light
of dawn touching the stones. I see them still
busying you with tubes and a mask, and me
trundling behind you across pleasant country.

There were rough kindnesses, the ministry
of sheets and cups, a quiet hand stretched out
in case you fell, as when our son was born
somebody washed my aching back with water.

You have come through. Your face is older now
you exercise, keep thin, you are more wary,
you say you prize your life higher than chocolate.
But when I talk with those whose men have died
I always see two labourers in the field
how one is taken and the other left
and no-one understands
why one must limp into the dark, the other
come staggering into unexpected light.

Artwork

The light stays perfect only for a short time, nearly always
the photographer, going for the sunset touch, sullenly stows
his gear back into the camper.
The milk-white child, cradled like water in his mother's arms,
stamps a hot foot.
New love, cooling, grows its first skin.

'The Light Stays Perfect only for a short time':
title of an exhibition of school artwork in Rheindahlen, Germany

66

Reading Edward Thomas in Celia's Garden

I think he would have understood this grief
this fear that Lad's Love will become Old Man,
he fell so often himself out of bright day
into cold forests where he lost his track
and himself and found he was nothing. I think he knew well
the death hours between startime and first light
when the bed is a pit and the body screams for release
into its next raw day. I think he knew this.

He particularly loved birds, the minute traceries
of their feet on winter roads, their brave mad singing
before the swoop of dark. He knew his flowers
with the intimacy of a lover. He had seen
dormice dine and seeds sprout amazingly
in nests where earth had settled. Always,
out of the bigger landscape, out of the hardness
of ice and wet and flailing wind, he plucked
some little glory. To him the kernel of earth
was ash-leaves shed on the road looking
like small black fish or a plain washed sky
that spoke hope to his anxious heart.

All these we gathered together like precious fruit and as day ended
we carried our chairs to the rosemary tree
to harvest the last warm drops lest the sun itself
should dissolve and take us too
down darkling ways to the forest where nothing is.

Friend, let us keep these things bright,
the psalm of the thrush, a robin's breast in the dark,
chirping against the cold, and the cold winter.